Contents

BRATZ™

Pedigree®

Published by Pedigree Books Limited, Beech Hill House,
Walnut Gardens, Exeter, Devon, EX4 4DH.
Email: books@pedigreegroup.co.uk

£7.99

JADE'S ATTITUDE TO FASHION MATCHES HER ATTITUDE TO LIFE – TOTALLY FAR OUT! HER STYLIN' FLAIR ALWAYS KEEPS HER AHEAD OF THE GAME, AND HER SASSY WIT MAKES HER A MATCH FOR ANYONE. KNOWN TO HER FRIENDS AS 'KOOL KAT', SHE'S DEFINITELY THE COOLEST FRIEND YOU COULD EVER WANT!

NICKNAME: KOOL KAT

FAVE COLOUR: GREEN

LUCKY NUMBER: 11

FAVE FOOD: ICE CREAM

FASHION PASSION: ANYTHING NEW AND FUNKALISH!

FAVE MUSIC: ALL STYLES, FROM RETRO NEW WAVE TO FUTURE FUNK

FAVE SMOOTHIE: STRAWBERRY

SHOPPIN' STYLE: THE COOLEST SHOPS AND THE HIPPEST STYLES

BEST BODY PART: LIPS

Yasmin ™

YASMIN'S FASHION PASSION IS FOR RETRO BOHEMIAN STYLE AND EARTH-TONE COLOURS. KNOWN AS 'PRETTY PRINCESS', SHE MAKES ANYTHING SHE WEARS LOOK LIKE SHEER ROYAL PERFECTION.

NICKNAME: PRETTY PRINCESS

FAVE COLOUR: AUTUMN SHADES

LUCKY NUMBER: 7

FASHION PASSION: BOHO RETRO COOL

FAVE MUSIC: CHILL-OUT GROOVES

FAVE FOOD: PIZZA

FAVE SMOOTHIE: APPLE

SHOPPIN' STYLE: BARGAIN HUNTER!

BEST BODY PART: HAIR

Sasha ™

COMBINING OL' SCHOOL ATTITUDE WITH NEW FUNK, WHEN 'BUNNY BOO' STRUTS HER STUFF SHE REALLY TURNS HEADS! IN HER LOVE OF MUSIC AS WELL AS HER PASSION FOR FASHION, SHE BRINGS TOGETHER THE HEYDAY OF HIP-HOP AND THE COOL OF R&B SOUL!

NICKNAME: BUNNY BOO

FAVE COLOUR: RED

LUCKY NUMBER: 3

BEST BODY PART: HANDS

FASHION PASSION: OL' SCHOOL AND NEW FUNK

FAVE MUSIC: HIP-HOP AND JAMMIN' SOUL

FAVE FOOD: COOKIES

FAVE SMOOTHIE: BLUEBERRY

SHOPPIN' STYLE: LOOKING OUT FOR STYLES TO SUIT ALL MY FRIENDS

Cloe

CLOE'S FUNKY STYLE INCLUDES EXOTIC ANIMAL PRINTS AND SPARKLING FABRICS – SHE'S KNOWN AS 'ANGEL' BECAUSE WHATEVER SHE WEARS, SHE MAKES IT LOOK DIVINE!

NICKNAME: ANGEL

FAVE COLOUR: TURQUOISE

LUCKY NUMBER: 6

FAVE SMOOTHIE: BANANA

FASHION PASSION: ANIMAL PRINTS AND SPARKLY FABRICS

FAVE MUSIC: POWER POP & GARAGE ROCK

SHOPPIN' STYLE: BEAUTY PRODUCTS AND GLITTERING MAKEUP

FAVE FOOD: WAFFLES

BEST BODY PART: NECK

Meygan ™

LAID BACK AND STYLIN', MEYGAN IS KNOWN AS 'FUNKY FASHION MONKEY' BECAUSE EVEN WHEN SHE'S JUST HANGIN' OUT, SHE STILL LOOKS GOOD.

NICKNAME: FUNKY FASHION MONKEY

FAVE COLOUR: PINK

LUCKY NUMBER: 1

FAVE SMOOTHIE: RASPBERRY

FAVE FOOD: FRUIT SALAD

FAVE MUSIC: POP

BEST BODY PART: EYES

Dana ™

DANA IS CALLED 'SUGAR SHOES'
BECAUSE SHE'S SO SWEET!

NICKNAME: SUGAR SHOES

FAVE COLOUR: PURPLE

LUCKY NUMBER: 2

FAVE MUSIC: CLASSIC ROCK

STAR SIGN: CANCER

FAVE FOOD: PASTA

BEST BODY PART: STOMACH

FAVE SMOOTHIE: MELON

Fianna ™

FIANNA REALLY HAS A NOSE FOR LOOKIN'
GREAT! SHE'S CALLED 'FRAGRANCE' BECAUSE
SHE'S AS SWEET AS SHE SMELLS!

NICKNAME: FRAGRANCE

FAVE COLOUR: GOLD

LUCKY NUMBER: 4

FAVE MUSIC: PUNK

FAVE FOOD: FRENCH TOAST

FAVE SMOOTHIE: PINEAPPLE

BEST BODY PART: SHOULDERS

Nevra ™

HEADSTRONG NEVRA IS KNOWN AS 'QUEEN B' BECAUSE SHE'S SWEET LIKE HONEY AND ALWAYS IN CHARGE – OF HER FASHIONS!

NICKNAME: QUEEN B

FAVE COLOUR: SILVER

LUCKY NUMBER: 5

FAVE MUSIC: 70S STYLE DANCE

FAVE SMOOTHIE: ORANGE

FAVE FOOD: RISOTTO

BEST BODY PART: BACK

Stylin' Profile

MY FAVE COLOURS ARE...

Blue *[handwritten]*

MY FAVE RETRO PERIOD IS...

MY FAVE FABRICS ARE...

[handwritten]

SO WHAT'S YOUR FASHION PASSION? EVERYONE HAS TO FIND THEIR OWN TRULY UNIQUE STYLE IF THEY'RE REALLY GONNA BE A FASHION QUEEN – COMPLETE THESE BOXES TO PROFILE YOUR OWN INDIVIDUAL STYLE!

MY FAVE TOP...

STAR STYLE – WHO DO YOU THINK ALWAYS LOOKS STYLIN'?

THE ITEM YOU ALWAYS GET COMPLIMENTS ABOUT?

I CAN'T BE WITHOUT...

MY TOP FIVE ACCESSORIES ARE...

MY FAVE TROUSERS OR SKIRT...

Mix 'n' Match

THE GIRLS HAVE BEEN LOOKING AT THEIR FUNKY NEW BOOTS AND NOW THEY'RE ALL MIXED UP! MATCH UP THE PAIRS TO FIND OUT WHICH GIRL HAS LOST ONE OF HER BOOTS.

Fashion on the Wild Side

Hi, I'm Sade, and I'm here to tell you that fashion isn't just fun - it's a lifesaver! We were totally freakin' about our school assignment, until our fashion sense came to the rescue! We always carry a camera with us - you never know when you're gonna need to snap someone! Have a look at our pics as you find out what happened!

We were all looking forward to our big girls' night out. We'd been planning it for a week, and we were still talking about it as we went into biology – the last class of the day. "Tonight's gonna be off the hook," said Sasha, brushing some cherry red lip gloss onto her full lips. "Nights out with you girls are the coolest."

"Don't forget we have to head for the mall after school," Cloe reminded them. "We've still gotta find the perfect outfits for tonight."

Yasmin smiled as she pulled out her textbooks. "For sure – shopping at the mall is almost as much fun as going out afterwards!"

"And there's a new boutique that's supposed to be totally hip," I added. We couldn't wait for the lesson to finish. But Mr Pearson, our biology teacher, was definitely about to change our mood!

Bling Bling BOUTIQUE

I was watching Cloe sketch a really cutting-edge tight fitting jacket and hipster jeans – we all love *Angel's* artistic flair – when Mr Pearson's voice broke into my thoughts.

"Tonight's assignment is to get closer to nature," he said. "Examine the natural world around you, and take some pictures of *Wildlife* to show the class tomorrow."

"But that leaves us no time to party!" groaned Yasmin under her breath.

"Or to blitz the mall!" I added. "What are we gonna do?" We spent the rest of the lesson in a daze, and when it finished we dashed out to meet Meygan and tell her the news. She was waiting for us by Cloe's blue and silver Cadillac, **brushing her silky red hair.**

"Hey ladies!" she called when she saw us. "You ready to flaunt it down at the mall?"

"Looks like the only thing we'll be flauntin' is our talent for photography," said Yasmin grimly. Meygan totally freaked when she heard about the assignment. "I can't believe he's ruining my night too – and I don't even do biology!"

"Come on y'all, time's a wastin'!" said Sasha. "Let's hit the mall anyway and try to figure something out while we're shoppin'".

brushing her silky red hair!

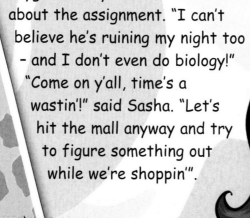

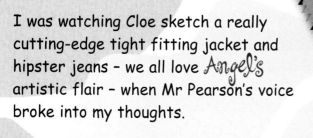

You can always trust _Bunny Boo_ to get practical! We hopped into Cloe's car and she got behind the wheel. As she glanced in the rear view mirror I caught her eye and I knew we were both thinking the same thing. What were we going to do? Cloe blinked her big crystal blue eyes and pulled out her mascara wand.

"After that lesson I need a really good facial in the spa," she sighed. "I heard their new mud mask is zingin'."
"We don't even have time to grab a smoothie!" exclaimed Meygan. "This is a total emergency!"
"Hey, de-stress girls!" called Koby, who was walking past the car with Dylan. But he looked stressed when he saw the glares we gave him!

"What's crackin'?" asked Dylan. "Last time I saw you, you were all excited about tonight!"
"Yeah," agreed Koby, "you wouldn't even listen to my latest film idea!" (Koby's an A/V wizard, and we have to show way too much interest in the freaky films he makes!)
"That was before Mr Pearson threw us a curve ball," explained Sasha. "We've gotta jet, guys, or we'll never figure out how to fix it!"
"Later, ladies, grinned Dylan. "Be cool!"

"Let's go, *Angel*" said Yasmin. Cloe flicked her long blonde hair back and the Cadillac purred smoothly out of school. At least we didn't have to catch the bus to the mall any more! Since Cloe got her vintage wheels, we've found a whole new kinda freedom!

"Anyone had any ideas?" I asked as we pulled onto the main road. "'Cause my mind's a blank."

"When is it not?" teased Sasha.

"Couldn't you just write us a really imaginative excuse, Yasmin?" said Cloe with a smile. Yasmin's got a real talent as a writer – although she's pretty shy about it too!

When we arrived at the mall we stepped out of the car and checked our reflections in our pocket mirrors. If you don't look good when you're hunting for new threads then nothing's gonna look good. Then we looked at each other with determination.

"Ok, ladies," said Sasha. "We've gotta get in there and locate the perfect looks! And if anyone has a brainwave about this stupid assignment – shout!"

"I'm gonna shout if we don't have a brainwave!" groaned Meygan.

We headed for the entrance, but we were totally lacking our usual buzz.

The clock was ticking, and if we didn't think of something, our girls' night out was gonna turn into a girls' nightmare!

We dived straight into our favourite boutique, Chix. Normally we'd have spent time scouting the other shops, checking out the newest ranges and giving ourselves plenty of smoothie breaks. But this was no time for fun – we were on a mission! We dashed around the shop, grabbing armfuls of clothes and trusting in our usual fashion sense to guide us. Then we regrouped in the changing room to look through our finds.

"This skirt would be slammin'," said Sasha through gritted teeth, as she held up a sparkling pink mini, "if we were headin' for a winter party!"
"Yeah," agreed Yasmin. "With a blue polo and long boots it'd be totally funkalish – but not for a girls' night out in the city!

"Here's a funky little retro top," exclaimed Meygan, holding up a green slash-neck tee. "It would look x-treme on you, Kool Kat."
"For sure," I replied, "But that's a wear-to-school top – I need something a bit wilder for a night out with my girls!"
As the minutes ticked away we got more and more stressed. I saw Yasmin pressing her glossy lips together hard – she always does that when she's nervous.

I was starting to panic too – nothing I tried on had that cutting-edge look I'm known for. Meanwhile the pile of clothes in the changing room was steadily growing and none of us could find one thing we liked.

"This is hopeless!" said Cloe in despair. "Shoppin's no fun when the pressure's on!"

Yasmin looked at our reflections in the full-length mirror and frowned.

"Girls, we need a lil' time out!" she said. "We can make anything fun – let's get outta here and find some smoothies. I know we'll think of something!"

We trooped out of the boutique, still feelin' low. Like Cloe said, it's tough to find the right clothes when you're stressed! We were heading for the smoothie bar when Meygan gave a yell and pointed to the machine by the glass lifts.

"A photo booth! Come on, y'all!"

"But Monkey, we've got a camera!" I said patiently.

"A photo booth isn't just about taking pics!" insisted Meygan. "We need to add a little fun to the mix!"

Meygan dragged us, protesting, over to the machine and into the booth. It was a pretty tight fit! Meygan, who was the last in, pulled the curtain across and fell over my lap. "I dropped the money!" she yelled.

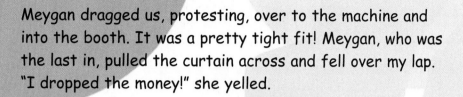

Bunny Boo You're sitting on my foot!" Cloe squealed in agony.
Get your knee outta my face!" growled Sasha.

"Someone's gotta move, 'cause I can't see a thing!" said Yasmin's muffled voice.

"I think I sat on someone's hand!" I giggled.

Then suddenly – we were all giggling!

"I'm at the wrong angle!" exclaimed Sasha. "It won't take my best side! Swap places, Princess?"

"This is the coolest!" said Cloe from the corner.

"Has anyone seen my feet?" asked Yasmin.

Meygan was still crawling around on the floor picking up the money she'd dropped.

"Don't make me laugh any more!" she pleaded, "I'll get the hiccups!"

Somehow we managed to find the money, get it into the machine and press the button.

"Best friends!" we yelled!

Flash! Flash! Flash! Flash!

By the time we had managed to squeeze out of the booth, we definitely had our old buzz back! Anything can be fun with your friends, right? Even last-minute assignments! We touched up our make-up while we waited for the photos to come out – my eyeliner had got badly smudged in the crush!

Then the pics dropped out of the machine and there was a rush to be the first to see them!

"You look really surprised in that one, *Angel*!" I grinned.

"Yeah," said Cloe, "That was when Sasha sat on my other foot!"

When we'd stopped giggling, Pretty *Princess* pointed down to the far end of the mall.

"There's that new boutique," she reminded us.

"Let's check it out!

The new boutique was painted in cool pastel shades and was playing some kickin' hip hop sounds – so I knew *Bunny Boo* would love it! Before we went in I took a look in the window – it's the best way to tell how up-to-the-minute a shop is!

There were some truly funky threads in the window display, so I was totally inspired to check it out. It had a really different look – and I love different!

As soon as we stepped inside I spotted a funkalish pair of cropped trousers in safari cream. A hip new look was definitely budding! I couldn't wait to try them on, but I knew I'd need a slammin' top to go with them.

Then I saw it! A stylin' lil' black top with criss-cross fastenings across the front. For the finishing touch I grabbed a thick black belt with gold studs and headed for the changing room. I knew this safari look would be totally ahead of the game!

Next into the changing room was Angel, smiling widely. She'd found a white and khaki strapless top, figure hugging and really cute. She had a pair of cool combats with a camouflage flare and a white belt that sat low and snug on her hips.

"Awesome, Angel!" I grinned. "You look cute and comfortable – the best ever combination!"
"What about this?" asked Meygan, her hands on her hips. Our smiles said it all! She'd found a lace-up top in fiery tiger colours that really toned with her glossy red hair and violet eyes. To set it off she'd picked out a pair of simple but stunning dark blue jeans and a thick silver and black belt. Effortless style, Fashion Monkey!

Suddenly our shoppin' trip was a blast! Sasha pulled on some super-stylin' hotpants and high leg boots, all in a kinda jungle print that was totally hip. A funky little bodice and neck scarf completed the perfect outfit.

"This music just makes me wanna dance!" she smiled, looking at her reflection.

Yasmin found a combat skirt and animal print boots that looked smoulderin' with a tight-fitting white tee.

"Always the style queen!" I grinned at her, and she struck a pose as I took a picture.

"It's getting a bit crowded in here!" she giggled, remembering the photo booth. We stepped out of the changing room to get a better look at our new outfits, and Sasha just couldn't resist the rhythm! We started dancing right there in the shop!

"Our girls' night out is just getting started!" Meygan grinned.

"But what about the assignment?" Cloe reminded us. That stopped us dancing – but nothing could bring us down from this high! "I know we'll think of something," Sasha said firmly. "We've just gotta put our heads together."

That's when I saw the shop assistant heading our way. I thought we were gonna get told off for dancing – but I knew this was a hip shop! She was smiling at us.

"I must say girls, you really make our new wildlife range look absolutely fantastic!" the assistant said. "I love the combinations you've chosen!"

"Thanks!" we chorused – all except Yasmin. She was staring at the shop assistant like she'd grown another head!

"What's up, Princess?" I asked.

"Don't you get it?" squeaked Yasmin in excitement. "It's the answer to our assignment!"

"What's the answer?" said Sasha impatiently.

"Wildlife!" exclaimed Yasmin, throwing her hands wide. "Look at us, ladies! Our outfits are totally inspired by nature! So let's give Mr Pearson some naturally cool pics of our new wildlife look!"

We all stared at Yasmin in amazed silence.

"I... I thought it was a good idea..." she stammered.

"Good?" exclaimed Angel, throwing her arms around Yasmin's neck and giving her a warm hug. "It's brilliant!"

"It's genius!" I added.

"Let's do it!" whooped Meygan.

Cloe

Jade

Yasmin

When the shop assistant realised what we were doing, she was totally amazing! She brought some funky animal prints out from behind the counter and we used them as backdrops for the shots. Then I grabbed my camera and we each posed for our photos. We took a couple of each of us – one for the assignment and one for us to keep! Then the shop assistant took a final pic of us all posing together.

The Girls

"I'd like a copy of that!" she smiled. "We'll put it up in the boutique to show how fantastic our clothes can look!" When we'd thanked her and paid for our new clothes, we dashed over to the Quick Develop Photo Lab. Within half an hour we had our pics! Our assignment was sorted!
"Just enough time to go home and get ready to hit the town!" grinned Sasha.
"I'm feelin' like a tiger on the prowl!" Meygan added.
    "I don't think we'll need much make-up tonight!" laughed Yasmin.
        "We've got a natural glow!

Megan

Sasha

So that's how we had the wildest girls' night out ever. And the assignment? We got straight As – naturally!

I'M ALWAYS ON THE CUTTING EDGE OF THE LATEST FUNKY THREADS - HERE ARE SOME OF MY BASIC FASHIONS DOS AND DON'TS!

jade's

Do know what suits you! It might look good on your best mate, but if you've got a different style then be true to it!

Do dare to be different! Unique is chic!

Do combine different textures and patterns for that Yasmin boho glam!

Do use your makeup to match your outfit.

Do look in the top fashion mags and check out what's on the catwalk!

Do identify your best features! If you know what you love about your body, you can totally use your fashion to make the most of it!

Fashion Tips

 **Don't** be confined by tradition! If you wanna wear boots with a prom dress, you go girl!

 **Don't** wear what other people say you should!

Don't forget your accessories! They can make or break a groovin' look!

Hot Tip

Not everyone knows what colours suit them best! Sit in front of a mirror wearing a high-necked white top, then hold different coloured fabrics up beside your face. You should be able to tell which colours really make you glow!

 **Stylin' Stomach** Show it off, girl! Get a little crop top on and put that toned tum on display!

Perfect Pins If you love your legs, show them off with minis and shorts. Make sure you keep them in top condition with lots of moisturiser!

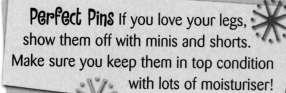 **Amazing Arms** Are your arms your best feature? Draw attention to them with floaty, shimmering fabrics and short sleeves.

Beautiful Back A low-backed dress will totally wow your friends! Dust glittery powder over your back for sparkling appeal!

Who's Your

DO THIS QUIZ TO FIND OUT WHICH GIRL IS YOUR FASHION FAVE!

My fave fashion era is

a) The 90s and that hip hop groove!
b) 70s boho.
c) 80s disco chic.
d) The latest hot catwalk trend!

My character is

a) Practical – a tower of strength.
b) Shy and sweet girl next door.
c) Creative and self-confident.
d) Daring and dramatic.

My fave colours are

a) Summer reds and yellows!
b) Winter frosty blues and whites.
c) Autumn greens and reds – earth colours!
d) Spring pastels.

My fave style is

a) Streetwise fashions that really stand out.
b) Classic clothes that never go out of style.
c) Vintage styles for retro-cool.
d) Cutting edge fashion that makes heads turn!

Fashion Fave?

My fave fashion shop is
a) Anywhere that sells the latest hip-hop trends.
b) The high street shops.
c) Second-hand clothes shops where you can pick up unique retro bargains!
d) That indie boutique you discovered on one of your fashion hunts!

My biggest nightmare is
a) No music.
b) No makeup.
c) No books.
d) No fashion.

Answers

Mostly a)s Sasha's your style guru!
Mostly b)s Cloe shares your passion for fashion!
Mostly c)s Yasmin would love your retro flair!
Mostly d)s You and Jade are always ahead of the game!

Fashion Fortune Teller

WE'RE ALWAYS ON THE PROWL FOR THE LATEST LOOK – KEEPIN' ONE STEP AHEAD OF THE CROWD! DO YOU THINK YOU'VE GOT WHAT IT TAKES TO BE A FASHION DESIGNER? USE THESE BOXES TO WRITE DOWN YOUR PREDICTIONS FOR THE YEAR'S MOST SUPERSTYLIN' FASHIONS. THEN CHECK BACK IN 12 MONTHS TO SEE HOW CLOSE YOU WERE!

The hottest fabrics are gonna be...

Everyone's fave retro era will be...

Everyone will be lovin' the colours...

The latest look in trousers will be...

The hippest tops will look...

Our groovin' accessories will be...

Skirts are gonna look...

And no wardrobe will be complete without...

Studying to Look Good!

THE GIRLS RULE THE SCHOOL WITH THEIR FASHION SENSE! HERE'S A GUIDE TO SOME FUNKALICIOUS LOOKS FOR EACH CLASS!

Maths

Maths
Your mix 'n' match talent adds up to great style!

English
We love reading – all the top fashion mags!

English

History

History
Fashion passions of the past!

Science

Science
We've got the formula for lookin' good!

Geography

Geography
Stiles High puts fashion on the map!

School Cool

Hi, I'm *Meygan*! Kick back and relax while I tell you all about the last day of school before the summer break. The girls thought it was going to be one big disappointment, until I came up with something to put the buzz back! It was top class!

We were in the assembly hall for the last time before the summer break – and everyone was in fever of excitement about the holidays. The last day of school is always a blast! We were together, as always, third row back – everyone always leaves those seats for us 'cause they know it's our spot! The boys strolled in and sat down behind us. Cameron leaned forward and put his hands on Cloe's shoulders in his usual friendly style.

"You ladies ready for a blazin' summer?"

"Totally!" said Jade. "And Miss Blight has given us a free period for the whole afternoon!"

"How do you girls always swing such x-treme luck?" grumbled Koby. "We've got double Biology with Mr Pearson!"

"Hard luck, Panther," I grinned, flicking back long hair. "I guess you didn't ace Biology like we did!"

Dylan leaned back with his hands behind his head and raised one eyebrow. In his funky chocolate brown sweater and cream combats, he looked ultra slick – although we weren't gonna boost his ego by telling him so!
Eitan and Cade started discussing their next surfin' extravaganza, so we switched attention back to our last-day-looks!

"I love your nail designs, *Kool Kat!*" whispered Yasmin as she examined Jade's stylin' nails. "Those tiny butterflies are groovin' – how did you manage to paint them so small?"

"I cannot tell a lie!" giggled Jade. "It was *Angel* – she came over last night and did them for me!"
"In return for a totally radical makeover!" Cloe grinned as we admired her skill.
"Could you do some for me too, Jade?" Yasmin begged.
"No worries," said Jade, "You can have mini gold crowns on a purple background!"

We were all about to demand personalised nail designs when Mr Stuart cleared his throat and stood up.
"Students!" he began. "We have reached the end of another long and rewarding year..."
I let his voice fade out as I flicked through the funky fashion mag Jade had brought in. I was looking at a cute little top with a pink heart corsage when I suddenly heard my name!

"Meygan"

Without thinking, I sprang to my feet and said "Sorry sir!" – but everyone started giggling! "Would you like to come up and collect your prize?" smiled Mr Stuart. It was the prize-giving ceremony and I had totally forgotten about it! I went up and collected my envelope, feeling my cheeks burning! When I got back to my seat, I found the girls quickly reapplying lipgloss and brushing their hair. "We don't wanna be caught out!" joked Sasha. I was checking my reflection in my little pocket mirror, when it was suddenly pulled out of my hand! I turned around to see Dylan checking his reflection and straightening his hair!

"Get your own mirror, Fox!" I laughed, taking it back from him. Nothing can embarrass Dylan though – he just gave me his usual cheeky grin and leaned back again. Sure enough, his was the next name to be called. I saw Koby and Cameron shaking their heads as Dylan sauntered up to collect his prize. By the end of the prize-giving, we had each been given a prize envelope.

"Let's open them over a few snacks?" suggested Jade, always hungry! We jetted down to the café and grabbed the big central table so we could all squeeze around it together – our lunchtime hotspot!

After we'd got a few plates of sharin' finger-food, we thought about what to do with our prize certificates.

"I'm gonna make a cute frame for mine," Cloe told us. "I found some stylin' sparkly material!"

"I'm gonna paste mine into my yearbook, along with pics of you guys!" said Yasmin.

"We should all make our own souvenirs of the last year!" Jade suggested. "But can we eat now?"

"Not until we've opened our prizes – together!" Cloe told her. "Everybody ready?"

We pulled out our prize envelopes and opened them at the same time – on the count of three!

There was a long silence.

"Definitely underwhelmed," said Sasha, staring at her certificate.

"Totally dullsville," Jade scowled.

"Do teachers have no imagination?" asked Cloe. "I don't wanna frame this!"

She shook the limp paper in the air crossly. The certificates were a lesson in how not to design! Just a white sheet of paper with tiny black writing! Not much of a prize after a year's hard studying!

"I've totally lost my appetite," Yasmin groaned, pushing her plate away.

"Those prizes suck," agreed Jade, helping herself to the rest of Yasmin's lunch.

"I wanted school to end on a real high!" wailed Sasha.

"I feel sorry for the boys," sighed Cloe, "cooped up in Biology this afternoon!"

I hated to see my friends so miserable! "Well I've got something to take your mind off Cameron!" I teased. "Be cool, ladies – the day's not over yet!"

"What are you plotting, girl?" asked Jade suspiciously.

"I've organised a treasure hunt for you all!" I grinned. "I've got your clues right here – first one to solve the clues will find the treasure – so the race is on!"

Everyone's face lit up immediately! We all love treasure hunts – Cloe had one at her last slumber party and it was the best fun, so I knew this was gonna be off the hook!

I handed out the first clues to my friends. They looked really stylin' – each one was on pink star-shaped paper and sprinkled with glitter! I'd arranged the hunt so each girl had her own set of clues to follow – a trail of pink stars around the school.

"This is awesome, Meygan!" squealed Cloe. "I love these pink stars! I want a corsage in just that shade of pink to go on my sparkly denim jacket!"

"You'd better get started on the clues!" I laughed. "They're not easy, you know!"

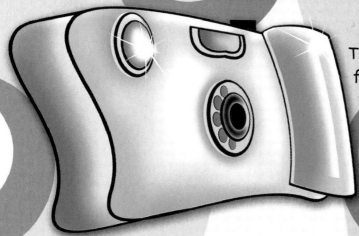

The girls were totally involved in figuring out their clues, so it was up to me to record the treasure hunt in our favourite way – photography! They decided to split up in different directions to make sure no one saw the others' clues. I decided to follow Sasha first.

"Let's see you pose, Bunny Boo!" I called, as she walked towards the playing fields. Her pink top and denim mini looked groovin' with her chunky sandals. She struck a pose but frowned as soon as the pic was snapped! "No more posing, Meygan – I have to figure out my first clue!"
She read it aloud:
"Your first clue
can clearly be seen
on the stylin' back
of a hip hop queen!"
Sasha read her clue out loud and glared at me.

Sasha

Your first clue
can clearly be seen
on the stylin' back
of a hip hop queen!

"What's that supposed to mean?"
"Hey, it wouldn't be any fun if it was easy!" I grinned, putting my arm around her (and sticking the next clue to her back! I wondered how long it would take for her to find it!). "I know you'll figure it out, Bunny Boo – but right now I have to see how Angel's doing!"

I found Cloe sitting in our form room, applying some glittery eyeshadow to her creamy eyelids.

"Funkalish colour, *Angel*!" I exclaimed, picking up the eyeshadow. It was a totally hot pale pink shimmer and it looked fantastic with her big blues.

"I was gonna ask if you wanted to borrow it for Dylan's party next week," she smiled – "depending on your outfit of course!"

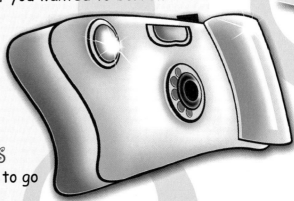

"Thanks!" I said, pulling out my camera. *Angel's* always so generous. "Now let's have a hot pose to go with your hot eye colour!"

Cloe struck a pose and I snapped her. She looked ready for the catwalk in her cool-for-school outfit – a figure-hugging pink and white tee with a violet skirt, set off with a low ponytail for total elegance!

"So have you worked out your clue already?"

"Are you kidding? This is really hard – I needed to face it with some hard-working make-up!

*"For a perfect Angel
With eyes of blue
This stylin' lady
Makes dreams come true!"*

Cloe

I shrugged. "Don't take too long, girl – Sasha's already thinking hard!" I knew it wouldn't take long for Cloe to think of the big mural of an angel she'd painted on the common room wall last year! I left her puzzling over her clue and went to find Yasmin.

For a perfect Angel
With eyes of blue
This stylin' lady
Makes dreams come true!

Your passion for fashion's
So retro cool
They even have
samples of it
in school!

Yasmin waved her pink star clue in the air as she saw me walking towards her.

"You could have made this a bit easier!" she called. "My brain doesn't wanna do any work on the last day of term!"

"Strike a pose, Pretty Princess!" I ordered. Yasmin let me snap her before turning back to her clue again.

She was totally cool in her favourite boho look – a pale blue strapless top with dark blue jeans and a co-ordinating wrap sitting lightly on her hips.

"Your passion for fashion's
So retro cool
They even have samples
Of it in school!"

Yasmin shrugged her shoulders expressively and shook back her light brown hair.

"Keep thinkin', girl, you'll get there!" I grinned. Yasmin squealed as I walked off and I realised that her quick brain had worked it out! Our school was built back in the 60s, which just so happens to be the era that's the main inspiration for Yasmin's funky retro style! There's always a bunch of really cool vintage fabrics in the art department, so that's where I hid her next clue! I watched her run off and went to find Jade.

Yasmin

On the way I saw Sasha dashing towards the tennis courts – she'd obviously solved her second clue:

"If you're feelin' sporty
Then where would you be
With a cute pleated mini
And a little white tee?"

If you're
feelin' sporty
Then where would you be
With a cute
pleated mini
And a little white tee?

A fashion pioneer
Who's feelin' groovy
Where does she go
For her favourite
smoothie?

Jade was pacing up and down outside the science lab. "Meygan, you gotta help me out here!" she laughed ruefully. "I haven't got a clue!"

"Yes you have – right there in your hand!" I joked. "Read it out loud, Jade, it might help!"

"A fashion pioneer
Who's feelin' groovy
Where does she go
For her favourite smoothie?"

I pulled out my camera and got a super-cool shot of Jade with her baffling clue! She always has a head-turnin' look, and for the last day of school she'd put together a cracklin' combo of a strappy cream top and slashed crop trousers, with a smoke-grey cap. No one does new like *Kool Kat*! I knew she'd soon crack her clue and head for the e-Café.

Jade

If you wanna keep secrets
Then this is the place
To hide
away photos
Of your crush's face!

Meanwhile Cloe had found her second clue on the mural and I was pretty sure she'd know the answer straight away –

"If you wanna keep secrets
Then this is the place
To hide away photos
Of your crush's face!"

Cloe won't even show us whose pic she keeps in her **school locker!**

Yasmin's next clue was a toughie:
"Koby thinks it's more fun
Than hittin' the mall
With pictures of Stiles High
On every wall!"
But I knew she'd get it of course – the
A/V workshop where Koby loves to hang
out! I stuck her final clue over a picture
of her that Koby had taken for the
school magazine!

Jade was gonna be finishing up
in the library if she got her
next clue right:
"A place of silence
So read my lips
There aren't enough books
With cool fashion tips!"

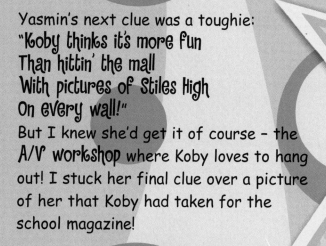

Koby thinks it's more fun
Than hittin' the mall
With pictures
of Stiles High
On every wall!

I watched them dashing around school. Soon each had
found the last clue – now they all had to work it out
and be the first to the treasure! But right now the
sun was scorchin' and I was definitely ready to
get into some shade! I had spent hours cookin'
up this treat for my
best friends, but that
didn't mean I had to get
sunburn for them too – we
all know that too much sun is
an enemy to glowing skin!

A place of silence
So read my lips
There aren't
enough books
With cool fashion tips!

Sun Block 15

If you can't hit the surf
And the sun makes you frown
Where's the next best place
For a babe to cool down?

The last clue was the same for each girl – and I wondered how long it would take for them to figure it out!

"If you can't hit the surf
And the sun makes you frown
Where's the next best place
For a babe to cool down?"

When the door to the **swimming pool** opened, I knew just what to expect! All four of my best friends had solved their clues – and arrived at the same time! As they burst through the door and saw me, their faces were totally worth the trouble! Linking arms and giggling, they came over to the edge of the pool where I sat, surrounded by prizes!

"I'm so out of breath!" Jade gasped. "After running around school all afternoon I need a smoothie!"

"You girls were super-fast!" I laughed. "I only just beat you here after taking all those pics!"

"That was totally cool, Meygan!" said Cloe, "but there's just one thing...?"

"Yes?" I asked.

"WHICH OF US WON?" they chorused!

"I just knew I wouldn't be able to answer that!" I told them.

"We've always been the best and the only ones who can compete with us - are us! Which is why I made sure there was enough treasure for everyone!"

"This rocks!" cried Jade, as she pulled out her prize – a stylin' new bikini!

"A manicure set – fantastic!" exclaimed Cloe.

Yasmin squealed in delight when she saw her prize – a funky journal decorated in genuine vintage fabrics! And Sasha utterly flipped over the CD I'd found in her favourite hip hop music shop.

Best friends

"That's not all!" I added, pulling out the certificates I'd made. "One pink star for each of you – officially the best friends ever!"

Class of

The winter ski trip

Cloe started the year lookin' hip

The high school prom!

Jade puts the style into Stiles High!

Fianna loved that spring term look!

Nevra got fashion inspiration from the school trip to Paris!

Dana lit up the 80's school disco!

Nevra looked x-tream on the geography field trip!

Cheering on the guys in the football team!

I KNOW ALL ABOUT KICKIN' BACK AFTER SOME HARD STUDYING – HERE ARE A FEW POINTERS TO HELP YOU MAKE THE MOST OF YOUR relaxation time!

Meygan's

A long soak in the bath – turn down the lights and use plenty of bubbles!

Beauty sleep – make sure you get plenty of sleep to keep your skin glowing and your eyes sparkling!

Music ambience – put your favourite sounds on the CD player and let your stresses float away!

Chill-out Tips

Exercise – if you're feelin' stressed, head for your local gym 'n' swim. Work that tension out of your body – and get toned at the same time!

Boudoir Bliss – your room should be a place you feel totally relaxed! Use colours and fabrics to decorate in your fave style.

Massage – Nothing relaxes your body like a deep-reachin' massage at the local salon!

Aromatherapy – Use joss sticks or incense cones to make your room really fragrant.

Slumber party – my top way to relax – chill out with good food and good friends!

Out!

Awesome! School's finished for the summer and I can pack away my textbooks. But can unscramble the letters to figure out which subjects I've been studying all year?

7.

N I
L E
S H G

8.

H R M
S C E
I T Y

9.

H A
S P
I
N S

Recipe for a Stylin' Makeup Bag

YOUR MAKEUP BAG IS A TOOL TO HELP YOU LOOK YOUR BEST! SO MAKE SURE YOU INCLUDE THESE ESSENTIAL BEAUTY AIDS!

Concealer – in case of unexpected blemishes

Eyeliner – define your peepers!

Neutral eye shadow – pick the colour that always looks fab on you!

Natural lip gloss – guaranteed to add effortless glam!

luscious lip gloss

Mascara – big lashes speak volumes!

Cotton buds/tissues – to fix mistakes!

Mini mirror – to check out your handiwork

Mini comb – to sort out those tangled tresses

Slammin' Smoothies

THE GIRLS WANT TO SHARE THEIR FAVOURITE SMOOTHIES WITH YOU! THEY'RE SUPER-SIMPLE TO MAKE. JUST PUT ALL INGREDIENTS INTO A BLENDER, BLEND UNTIL SMOOTHIE CONSISTENCY IS REACHED AND SERVE IN TALL GLASSES!

Strawberry Smoothie

5 large strawberries
6oz strawberry ice cream
4 oz lemonade
2 teaspoons of sugar

Banana Smoothie

1 medium banana
1 cup skimmed milk
1 cup vanilla ice cream
2 teaspoons sugar

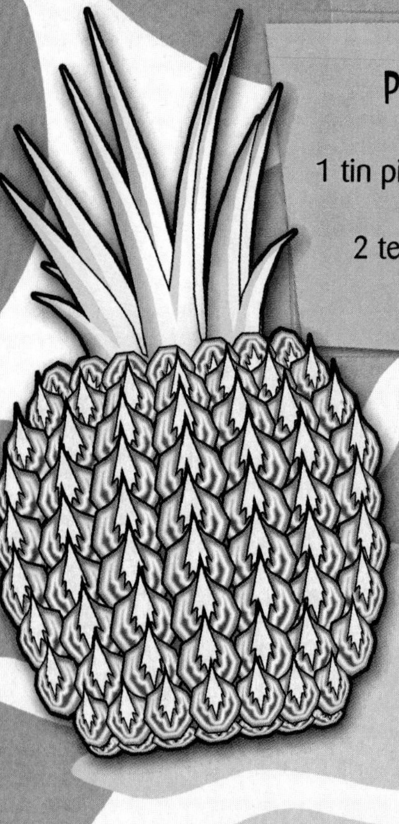

Pineapple Smoothie

1 tin pineapple chunks and juice
1 cup milk
2 teaspoons vanilla extract
2 teaspoons sugar

Orange Smoothie

6oz orange juice
1 cup milk
1 cup water
2 teaspoons sugar
1/2 teaspoon vanilla extract
Ice cubes

Hi, I'm Yasmin, and I'm gonna show you just what a killer combo of best friends and stylin' wardrobes can achieve! When it comes to fashion emergencies, my girls and I can solve anything!

We were all over at Jade's house, lounging around her funky room and chatting. Jade was using the tongs on Cloe's hair – with curls she looks even more angelic! I was giving Sasha's nails a French polish and we were all discussing the party that we were preparing for. We couldn't wait! Dylan had been planning it for weeks – a really sizzlin' festivity to celebrate the end of school and the start of summer! At last the big night was here, and we were gonna make sure we looked the best – just like we always do! Glowing looks and stylin' fashion take plenty of time and dedication!

"I'm gonna focus on a kinda beach look," Sasha said. "After all, the theme is 'stylin' summer' and there's nothing that says summer like a funky fringed beach dress!"

"Hot idea, Bunny Boo," agreed Jade. "But I'm planning something a bit unusual!"

"No surprises there then!" I teased. Jade's always out front with her fashion sense. Lookin' around her room it's easy to see that this is the domain of a real style queen!

"I'm thinkin' a hot Latin look," Jade mused, "with fire-coloured silks and satins, and killer heels!"

"That'll look sizzlin' with your black hair, Kool Kat," said Cloe. "I've got a couple of crimson fabric roses you could twist into your locks for a finishing touch!"

Fianna was lying on her stomach on Jade's bed, and she rolled onto her side to join in the conversation. "I'm gonna wear that fringed green bodice and cropped trousers combo I bought in the mall last week," she said. "With strappy sandals it's definitely the image for the summer!"

"That'll look totally hip, girl," I agreed. "What about you, Angel?"

Cloe smiled dreamily. "I'm going with the hot summer idea too," she told us. "A creamy animal-print mini with a sparkly turquoise halter neck and some funky shades."

"We're gonna have the hottest looks at the party!" I said.

"We always manage to stand out!" agreed Fianna.

"So what are you gonna wear, Princess?" asked Cloe. But I wasn't destined to tell them! Because that's when the phone rang – and changed everything!

Jade stretched out her arm lazily to grab the phone – like all of us, she has it by her bed so it's always in easy reach. It was Dylan.

"Hey Fox, what's up?" she smiled. "Mind if I put you on speakerphone?"

"No worries," we heard Dylan say as Jade pressed the conference call button on her phone. "Evening, girls!"

"Ladies!" we yelled together! Dylan just laughed.

"I'm just callin' to make sure you're all gonna scamper over to my party tonight? It wouldn't be a party without you there!"

"Hang loose, we'll be there," Sasha called. Then we heard Cameron say something in the background.

"Was that the Blaze?" asked Cloe.

"Oh yeah, one more thing!" said Dylan, suddenly sounding a bit hot and bothered. "I forgot to mention it last week, but I - er - changed the theme of the party."

"You what?" we screamed.

"It's gonna be a flashback theme – a rockin' retro flavour – gotta jet – see ya later!"

We shrieked but he had already hung up the phone! We stared at each other in horror. The party was just a couple of hours away and the mall was shut – what were we gonna do?

Even cool-headed Sasha was panicking! **Talk about a fashion disaster!** It had taken us weeks of planning to come up with the perfect outfits, and now we had just two hours to start all over again!

"I've gotta go home and blitz through my wardrobe!" exclaimed Fianna, springing to her feet. "Stay in touch, ladies – mobiles ON!"

We all had the same idea! Cloe gave us a lift in her Cadillac, but for once we were too stressed to enjoy the ride!

"I just know I don't have anything!" wailed Fianna as we pulled up outside her house. "I think I've got a vintage 70s skirt from last summer, but that's it!"

"Think positive!" I called after her as she dashed up to her house.

When we reached Sasha's home she sprang out of the car without even opening the door!

"Hey!" yelled Cloe. "Watch the paintwork, girl!"

"Sorry *Angel*!" Sasha called over her shoulder. "But I don't know if I'm gonna make it – my wardrobe doesn't provide for retro!"

Cloe stepped on the gas and skidded to a halt outside my house.

"Later, *Princess*!" she called as I hopped out. "Let me hear from you!"

I dashed inside and straight up to my room, where I rifled through every drawer and wardrobe, searching for the right outfit! I knew I was the most likely to find a vintage look, 'cause I'm totally into the boho blend, but that doesn't mean I can put together a hip outfit with no warning! The heat was definitely on!

I was pulling a couple of floaty tees out of my drawer when the phone rang – it was Sasha.

"I'm freakin'!" she yelled. "What's the matter with Dylan? He knows we need time for something like this!"

"I guess that with all the other things he was organising, he just forgot," I sighed. But Sasha wasn't in a forgiving mood!

"I'm gonna give him a piece of my mind!" she snapped. "If I make it to the party! Jade just called me – she can't find anything that will make a retro outfit!"

"She's got that totally hip 80s belt," I remembered.

"A belt's no good without the clothes!" groaned Sasha. Just then my mobile started to ring.

"I gotta go, Bunny Boo – Cloe's callin' my moby!"

"Laters!" Sasha hung up and I grabbed my mobile.

58

"Hey Princess, what can I do with a 70s fringed shawl and a pair of platforms?" wailed Cloe's voice.

"Sasha and Jade are having trouble too," I told her. "And I can't find anything that will make a blazin' vintage statement. We're cooked!"

"Fianna can only find an Indian cotton drawstring top," Cloe added. "This is officially a disaster!"

"Keep lookin'," I told her hopefully. "I haven't skimmed through all my clothes yet – there might be something we haven't thought of!"

But when Cloe rang off I looked around my room in despair! I could see nothing that might save the situation – it looked like we'd be missing the fun! You can't rock up to a theme party and ignore the theme!

I thought of my friends doing exactly the same thing as me – trying to come up with a funky look with no time and no inspiration! It made it worse that we weren't even together... and that's when I had my big idea! I was on the phone to Jade like lightning!

"Hey girl! I've thought of something that just might save us! Get your entire wardrobe together and jet over to my house – no time to waste!"

"My entire wardrobe?" repeated Jade in shock. "But Princess–"

"Time's a wastin', Kool Kat!" I buzzed. "Call Cloe and tell her the same – I'll get onto Fianna and Sasha. Hurry!"

I rang Fianna and Sasha with the same message. If I was right, we would be able to solve our problem – but time was running out!

57

Soon I heard Cloe's car horn blasting outside – and when I looked out of the window I couldn't help but laugh! She had collected the other girls, and they had all done as I asked. **The car was so piled with fashion, I** couldn't even see the others! Cloe waved up at me with a grin – she was almost buried under a funky scarlet jacket of Jade's! I went out to help them and saw Sasha and Fianna emerge from under a mountain of minis!

"That was the scariest ride of my life!" gasped Jade, flinging jumpers to one side and staggering out of the car.
"It was totally hilarious!" giggled Fianna. "Cade saw us driving past and couldn't believe his eyes!"
"Yeah," Cloe laughed, "he couldn't see the other girls and he thought the clothes were calling his name!"

We gathered armfuls of clothes and jetted up to my room. It took us three trips each to get all the clothes from the car! Finally the other four collapsed onto my bed.
"Well?" asked Jade, raising her eyebrows.
"What's the scheme?" Sasha added.
"Be patient, o stylin' ones, all will become clear!"

I struck a pose and waved an arm at all the clothes.

"We tried to find retro outfits, but it was a total nightmare, right?"

"Ain't that the truth!" sighed Sasha. "So we team up!" I exclaimed. "Best friends like us can do anything when we're together! We'll go through our wardrobes and mix n' match everyone's fashions to make five truly funky styles!"

"You're not just a pretty face, *Princess*!" Jade exclaimed. "Let's do it!"

"We should pick out anything with a retro flavour," I suggested. "Then we can see what we've got to work with!"

So we dived in! After a few wild minutes Cloe sat back on her heels and blew her hair out of her eyes.

"I've found a few things that could look definitely retro!" she said triumphantly.

"*Princess*, you've got some awesome vintage patterns in here!" Sasha grinned, holding up my navy blue bikini with diagonal rainbow stripes.

"Not quite right for Dylan's party though, *Bunny Boo*!" I laughed, grabbing the bikini and throwing it back in the drawer. "Everyone ready?"

"How about this polka dot mini?" suggested Jade. "Totally 80s!"

61

"Wait a minute – I just saw something that screamed Fianna!" cried Cloe, pulling out a pair of toffee and white striped flares that sizzled with 70s funk fever!

"These are so retro cool!," I stated.

"They'd look groovin' on you, Fianna!" A tan leather belt added style, and picked out the brown in the trousers.

"Here's the ideal combo!" Jade grinned. She'd found a totally cool gypsy top in burgundy, with medieval sleeves and toffee-coloured detail at the elbows – way radical!

Fianna

"I've found some shoes that would exactly match that toffee stripe!" added Sasha.

"And for the finishing touch!" I flourished, tying a thin burgundy choker around Fianna's neck. The outfit was created!

"Your hair should be simple and stylish," added Cloe. Angel's a hair wizard! With a few quick flicks of the curling tongs she gave Fianna a funky 70s hairstyle!

"My turn!" cried Sasha, plucking a mint-green crop top from the pile. It had wide three-quarter length sleeves and a plunge v neckline.

"**Saturday night fever!**" Jade giggled. "We're talking glam, girls!"

Here's a jazzy little skirt!" said Fianna, pulling out an emerald green mini with a thick waistband.

"And these shoes are the real deal!" I added, locating my sunshine yellow heels with pretty side bows. "I got them from a vintage clothes agency!"

Sasha looked like a disco queen! A pair of gold earrings and silky flowing locks completed the image!

Sasha

Then Cloe held a long white boot up in the air. "Anyone find a match for this?"

"Me!" said Jade. "They've got that 60s mod beat that's so hot!"

"Definitely a look for you, *Kool Kat!*" laughed Cloe, passing the boot over. Sasha held out a stylin' white mini-dress that looked like it was made to match the boots!

With black fishnets and a funky purple and gold belt, Jade looked ultra mod – totally 60s cool! Cloe grabbed the ceramic hair straightener and made Jade's hair swing like a gleaming black curtain.

Jade

63

I had already seen the outfit I wanted to wear – a pair of purple hotpants with a zip top in white and red.
"But I don't know what shoes to wear!" I panicked. Jade came to the rescue! She pulled out a pair of ol' style roller boots – with knee-length rainbow-striped hold-ups and a pink sun visor, I was the image of the roller-boogie 80s!

Yasmin

Only one outfit left to find! Cloe picked out a black razzle-dazzle skirt with stiff netting that made it stand out.
"80s pop star!" she giggled.
"We need layers!" I instructed. We soon found a couple of vest tops and a little white choker that showed off Cloe's pretty neck. Then Sasha added some fishnets with the feet cut out and Jade wrapped a long silver crucifix necklace around Cloe's waist like a belt. With strappy heels she grabbed that totally awesome 80s look!

Cloe flicked out the ends of her hair with curling tongs and we lined up in front of the full-length mirrors to check our reflections.
"Girls, we are definitely fashionistas!" laughed Jade. "Your idea was a total triumph, Yasmin!"
"Just enough time to do our makeup!" Fianna reminded us.

Cloe

Cloe went for dazzling white eye shadow that really emphasised her blue eyes. I concentrated on making my lips look full and luscious with a damson lip gloss. Fianna continued her pink and purple theme with her makeup and a pink hair ribbon. Jade chose purple liquid eye colour to highlight her green eyes and Sasha picked a warm cherry lip colour. At last we were ready!

"I never thought we'd do it!" gasped Fianna as we did a final makeup and accessories check.

"Hey girl, we can do anything!" Jade told her, turning to Cloe. "Let's hit the road, hot wheels!"

We squeezed into the Cadillac and were soon speeding towards the party. Dylan's house looked x-treme! There were garden lights sprinkled along the edge of the path and Chinese lanterns hanging around the outside of the house! Inside, Dylan had decorated each room in the style of a different decade! It looked totally off the hook!

"Welcome, ladies!" cried the Fox when he saw us.

"We should be furious with you!" Sasha said, waggling her finger at him.

"But we forgive you," added Cloe.

"We had the best fun solving the problem!" Fianna giggled.

"Well whatever you did, you're lookin' hot!" he said, winking at us. "Come and grab yourselves a fruit cocktail!"

The party was a blast! There were some awesome retro fashions on the scene, but we were the ones who really stood out – thanks to our funkalish teamwork!

THERE'S NOTHING US GIRLS LIKE BETTER THAN A SUPER-SLAMMIN' PARTY! HERE ARE SOME TIPS TO MAKE SURE YOU HAVE A KICKIN' TIME.

Yasmin's

Dress to impress

Work out what you're gonna wear in advance and make sure you're totally in love with your outfit – if you know you look good, it'll make you sparkle!

Makeup mistress

Put your makeup on after your outfit, so you don't smudge it! Co-ordinate your colours and don't forget to take your makeup bag with you to the party – you might need to reapply gloss or eyeliner! Don't forget your phone

Party Tips

Friends

Any party is ten times more fun with your best friends there! Pick someone's house to get ready at and you'll be enjoying yourself before you even hit the party!

Music and dancing

You gotta strut your stuff, dancing queen! Feel the beat and start movin'! Don't forget to drink plenty of water or fruit cocktails while you're dancing – you need to rehydrate!

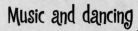

Be confident!

If you've got the perfect outfit, the perfect makeup and the perfect friends, what's not to love? Get in there and enjoy yourself, girl!

Don't be caught out when you have a last-minute outfit to organise! Use the mannequins to design a few stylin' party looks!

Xpress

RETRO

GET TOTALLY INSPIRED BY THESE FUNKALISH SNAPSHOTS OF PAST FASHIONS!

50's - Polka dots, feminine floaty fabrics, flat shoes, knee-length full skirts, pedal pushers, ponytails!

60's - Hippie, boho, floaty fabrics, bright colours, flower power, long hair!

FUNK

70's - Rainbow patterns, stripes, flares, white suits, big collars, platforms!

80's - Bows, batwings, layers, neons, netting, legwarmers, bright and colourful makeup!

69

Girls' Nite Out

Hi, I'm Cloe, and I want to tell you about a day during summer break when fashion wasn't enough! We were so excited about the big party, we forgot to read the small print!

"Have you opened yours?" Jade squealed down the phone at top volume.

"I assume you mean this *totally awesome invite!*" I crowed. We had all been invited to the party of the *season* – it only happens once a year and it's strictly invitation only!

"This calls for some ultra-hip fashion," buzzed Jade. "Let's hit the mall, Angels!"

After I picked up the girls we headed for the mall and went straight into Chix to start the day in our favourite boutique. I was checking some retro patterns when Jade flipped out!

"This is xtreme!" she yelled. She dashed into the changing room and came out in a shocking-pink two-piece outfit. The hipster flares were definitely catwalk cool! Jade had added a stylin' gypsy belt of gold coins that sat low on her hips.

"With black heels and some killer gold jewellery, that's gonna be *hot!*" Sasha grinned.

"I'm seriously crazy about this look!" agreed Jade. "Definitely my first purchase. But I'm not sure it's right for the party – I'm gonna keep looking!"

Dana fell in love with a little mini dress and plunged into the changing room. We don't call Dana 'Sugar Shoes' for nothing! She made that dress look totally sweet. It was a pale dusty pink with a flick out hem, and strapless so it showed off her glowing tan.

"I think I just found my party outfit, ladies!" Dana grinned.

"Don't speak too soon – we've got a load of shops to see yet!" smiled Yasmin.

"And we need to stay refreshed!" Jade added. "Let's pay for these and grab some smoothies!"

We jetted over to the smoothie bar and ordered our favourite flavours.

"I can't wait for this party to start!" giggled Dana, sipping her melon smoothie through a straw and trying not to smudge her lip gloss.

"It's ok for you, Sugar Shoes, you've found your outfit!" I exclaimed.

"Everyone says this party's gonna be off the hook," Jade sighed happily.

"What's the exact venue – I was so freaked by the invite I forgot to check!" asked Dana.

It turned out that we had all totally forgotten to check the address!

"No worries," I told them. "I'll look at it when we get back – I'll have to make sure I know how to drive there!"

luscious
lip gloss

Yasmin

The smoothies gave us the boost we needed to hit the shops again! Yasmin dragged us straight into her favourite retro haven and immediately saw a pair of 70s-style hipster blue jeans. She matched them with a vintage rainbow snake-clip belt and a floaty silk turquoise top that shimmered as she moved. *Princess* was hopin' to find something more sizzlin' for the party, but she knew she'd regret it if she didn't buy that outfit!

Just as we were about to leave, I saw a hip little green and red striped tee that I just *had* to have! I had been looking for a tee to go with my indigo hipster pedal pushers – **I really dig that 50s style**! With red bangles and black sandals, I knew I'd struck the look!

Cloe

Sasha

In a corner boutique Sasha found just what she was looking for!
"Are you ready to be impressed?" she called from behind the changing room curtain.
She wasn't kidding! She'd picked out a little red bandeau top and a dark blue mini in slinky velvet that was totally cutting edge fashion.
"Awesome, *Bunny Boo*! That's gonna definitely turn heads at the party!" grinned Jade.

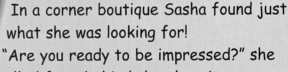

We went to try on some shoes and I picked up some cute strappy turquoise heels, while Dana found some pink clogs that would look radical with her new dress. Then we hit Fortuna, our favourite accessories shop. Even the hottest outfit can be improved with a little inspired accessorising! Dana and Sasha hovered over cute velvet clutch bags, while I picked out some stylin' hair clips and ties. You've gotta think of every aspect of your look – especially for an ultra-hip party like this one!

"Ribbons are definitely hot property this summer," Jade mused, sorting through the latest range. "Have you clocked my new ribbon-tie shoes, Angel?"

"They're definitely *one step* ahead!" I joked, and Jade rolled her eyes! But I meant it – Jade's latest footwear was totally stylin' – pink wedge heels that fastened around her ankles with crossover dark pink ribbons. Whatever Jade's wearing, you'll see it on the catwalk the following week!

Jade wanted to check out a new indie shop that had opened a few days ago. It didn't take her long to locate a groovin' little dress in powder-blue silk. She added a black leather jacket with a high collar and a red belt tied loosely at the waist. Jade had found her party image!

In the next boutique I found a **classic-cool look that felt like style royalty!** A tan suede mini with dark leather trims in a boho pattern, with knee-length white boots and a black satin body-hugger tee! I struck a pose and Dana snapped my pic.

"It's all the funk!" confirmed Jade.
"If ya got it, flaunt it!" I crowed!
Within minutes I was changed and standing at the counter to pay for my new duds. But suddenly Yasmin gave a squeal and darted back among the clothes!
"She's finally flipped!" laughed Sasha.
"Girl, have you tweaked?" called Jade. There was a silence, then Yasmin came out of the changing room and gave a proud twirl.

"You look amazing!" admired Dana. Yasmin certainly lived up to her nickname – she glowed like a *Princess!* She'd donned a funky royal blue mini, paired with a charcoal v-neck crop tee that had cute ties hanging from the shoulders.
"You could borrow my charcoal platform sandals," I offered. "They'd match that tee perfectly!"
"Let's *do* it already!" Jade hustled. "Two hours left to beautify!"

Cloe

At my house we laid out our purchases and makeup, and got ready to decide on our beauty schemes! I decided that I was gonna work on my peaches-and-cream complexion to give myself the angelic look I'm famous for. Half an hour before the party was due to start, I remembered that we hadn't checked the address yet. So while the others argued over brushes and colours, I went to check on the location.

"I'm gonna use this Light-Beam glow to give my cheeks a funky shimmer," Sasha announced, seizing the Light-Beam pot from under Dana's hand!
  "Watch it, girl!" responded Dana, waving a blush brush at Sasha warningly.
  "Has anyone seen my makeup sponge?" asked Jade, scrabbling through the piles of makeup on my dressing table.
"Sure you haven't *eaten* it, Kool Kat?" teased Yasmin.

That's when Sasha noticed how quiet I was.
  "Hey girl, what's crackin'? You look like you've seen a ghost!"
  I tried to speak, but I couldn't find the words! I handed the invitation to the girls.
"Soooo... it's the invite..." said Jade slowly.
  "Remember how none of us checked the small print for the party address?" I stammered.
    The girls nodded. "Well it's an hour's drive away!"

"Oh NO!" everyone screamed!
We stared at our watches in sheer horror. This was scarier than one of Sasha's ghost stories! We hadn't even finished our makeup and now we were in danger of totally missing the party!

"We can't be late for the coolest party of the year!" said Dana miserably.
"It's gonna take us at *least* half an hour to do our hair and makeup," added Yasmin, checking her watch again. "What are we gonna do?"
"Hire a helicopter?" said Jade wildly. Even in our panic we had to giggle at that! And the release of tension set Sasha's practical mind working.
"Aren't we all style divas?" she demanded. "If we have to **makeup on the move**, that's just the way it's gotta be!"
"What do you mean, *Bunny Boo*?" asked Yasmin.
"I mean that Cloe's Cadillac is gonna turn into a mobile stylin' salon," Sasha explained. "Let's jet, ladies – we need mirrors, makeup and cordless curling tongs!"
"Not to mention proper lighting!" I exclaimed, grabbing a battery-powered lamp. "Quick thinking, Sasha – if we start now we'll only be half an hour late!"
"And that's totally forgivable!" Jade crowed. "Let's do it!"

We swept all the makeup into an empty boutique bag and darted down to the car. As I sped out of the drive the girls started work on their makeup! Sasha held up the mirror and Yasmin grabbed the light, while Dana and Jade went to work on their war paint! Then they swapped places so Sasha and Yasmin could get dazzlin'! I hit the accelerator and we were soon powering along the back road to the party. It wasn't easy for the girls, putting on their makeup as I rounded the curves!

"Take it easy, Angel!" yelled Bunny Boo. "My lip liner just became my eye liner!"

"Sorry!" I giggled. "Just trying to get there, girl!"

"Finished!" grinned Yasmin triumphantly. "We're a style team!"

"Not quite!" Jade exclaimed, waggling the curling tongs under Yasmin's nose. "We still need a bit of hair flair!"

The road was getting bumpier as Jade went to work with the tongs.

"This party's really out in the sticks!" I commented, exchanging glances with Jade in the rear view mirror. "Hey, don't forget about my locks, Kool Kat!"

"I guess that's what keeps it exclusive," Jade replied, adding flick curls to my silky blonde hair. "You can only find it if you've been invited!"

Suddenly there was a horrible coughing sound from the engine!

The Cadillac started to spasm!
"What's happening?" squealed Dana.
"Quit foolin', *Angel*!" Jade snapped as the curling tongs flew out of her hand.
"Who's foolin'?" I groaned, looking down at the fuel gauge. "We're fried, girls! I'm outta petrol!"
The car slowed to a stop and we all sat in horrified silence for a moment. Just when we thought everything was gonna be okay! I opened the door and got out onto the road, looking for lights – any sign of a house nearby!

Dana

"We haven't passed any houses for miles," said Jade, getting out of the back and standing beside me. "I'll bet there's nothing for miles ahead, either."
"Another car is bound to come past sooner or later!" said Yasmin, poking her head out of the window.
"Not likely, *Pretty Princess*," Sasha sighed. "We're late for the party, remember? Everyone else is already there."
"Not everyone," said Dana firmly, joining us on the road. "Koby's never been on time for anything in his life. He's definitely gonna be lagging, girls, and for once it's gonna work in our favour!"
We looked at Dana doubtfully. It's true that Koby's well-known for being last-minute, but I couldn't believe he'd roll up late for *this* party!

Sasha was thinking the same thing.

"Even Koby won't have made delays for this groove," she said, shaking her head. "We're gonna have to call the breakdown service, *Angel*."

"But it'll take them ages to get here!" Yasmin cried. "We'll totally miss the party!"

"What do you suggest we do, *Princess*, walk?" snapped Sasha.

"Hey, no squabbling," I insisted. "We're gonna get through this by teaming up, not arguing!"

"It doesn't matter anyway," said Jade, holding her mobile up in the moonlight. "No signal! We can't phone the breakdown service or Koby!"

I tapped my foot impatiently on the uneven road. "This is turning into a nightmare!" I said. "No phones, no fuel and no party!"

"Why didn't you think to fill up with petrol before we left?" grumbled Dana.

"Why didn't any of you remind me?" I retorted.

"It's *your* car!" Jade snapped.

That's when Yasmin really pulled us together!

"Hey, girls," she said, with her radiant smile. "Even if the evening's ruined, that doesn't mean we have to get twitchy and fall out! Nobody's hurt, right? And we're all together – which means *we can make anything fun!*"

81

I started to feel better! Yasmin was right –
with your best friends around, there's no such
thing as a total disaster.
"I'm really sorry," I said. "I should have
thought about petrol."
"We *all* should," Jade replied, giving me a hug.
"I'm sorry I snapped."
"I guess we'll just have to party right here!"
shrugged Sasha.
"*Very exclusive!*" Dana giggled.

I leaned into the car to put some music on,
when Yasmin gave a yell.
"Perhaps not! I see lights!"
We all peered down the road – a pair of
headlights was winding slowly towards us!
"We're saved!" cheered Sasha. "A car!"
We stood in the middle of the road and
waved crazily at the car. It stopped in front of us
so we were blinded by the lights! Then we heard a familiar voice.
"You ladies in trouble?"
"Koby!" we shrieked, rushing over to him. He got out of his car and grinned at
us, his eyes twinkling.

Yasmin

"We've run out of petrol!" I explained with
relief. "We thought we were stuck here!"
"No problem," Koby replied with his
easy grin. "I've got a petrol can in
the boot for emergencies like
this!"
"And I'm gonna do the same
from now on!" I vowed.

Within minutes we were back on the road and following Koby up the winding road, and after another half hour we pulled in beside the country house where the party was being held.

Koby waved to us as he got out of his car. "I'll see you in there!" he called. "I'm late again – but this time I've got an excuse!" "I knew we'd pull it off!" grinned Kool Kat, hopping out of the Cadillac and checking her makeup in the wing mirror.
"We always do!" Yasmin said with a wink.
I grabbed the big mirror and Dana held it up while I did my makeup – as the driver I hadn't had chance! I quickly blended shimmering highlighter into my pink cheeks and slicked on cherry lip liner and gloss for a really kissable pout.
"Lookin' heavenly, Angel!" approved Dana.

"I think we should make an entrance to remember!" suggested Sasha. We linked arms and flung open the entrance door. There was a jumping music mix and I knew Sasha couldn't wait to start the dancing! Neither could I, for that matter! We looked at each other in appreciation – now we had arrived, the party of the year could really get started!

LOOKIN' GOOD MEANS FEELIN' GOOD –
HERE ARE SOME OF MY FAVE BEAUTY TIPS
FOR YOU TO TRY OUT!

Cloe's

Know your skin
Work out your own skincare routine! Everyone's different, so your cleansing, toning and moisturising routine has to be right for your skin.

Fantastic Facials
I'm a big fan of a really zingin' facial! It'll deep cleanse your pores and make you feel as fabulous as you look!

Nails
Have regular manicures and pedicures. Learn how to do them yourself and treat your friends! The beauty's in the detail! Little fingernail artwork or designer hairstyles will be sure to get you remembered!

Beauty Tips

Hair

I'm lovin' avocados – not only do they make a fantastic facial mask, they are also great for shiny hair! Mash up an avocado with a tablespoon of olive oil and a dash of baking powder. Mix it together well the work it into your hair. Wash out after 15 minutes for soft, shiny locks!

Experiment – you'll find out what works well and what looks fabulous! Try using different coloured hair clips or ribbons to create unique looks for your hair! You've never looked so funkalicious!

Eyes

Pick colours to bring out your natural beauty. If you're not sure which colours really suit your eye colour, here's a quick guide!

Blue eyes

In the daytime stick with deep blue, purple, violet or grey. For a funky evening dazzle try silver, turquoise or shocking pink!

Green/Hazel eyes

For daytime chic go for brown, forest green or plum. To jazz it up for a party look experiment with gold, lime green or bright purple.

Brown eyes

Your eyes will always suit copper, bronze, brown and khaki green. Your party peepers will look groovin' with royal blue, hot pink or orange.

Eyeliner – for big eyes draw a dark line starting from the middle of your lash line to the outer edge. Use a light coloured eye pencil and draw a line under the lower lash.

Hot Tip

Heat your eyelash curlers with your hair dryer for a few seconds. It's like curling tongs for the eyes!

Lips

Always prepare your lips with a slick of lip balm to keep them soft and kissable!

Lip liner is totally optional, but if you use it, it should go on first. Use a neutral colour or a liner that exactly matches your lipstick.

To make lips look fuller, line them with pencil then blend the edges with your finger. Cover with Vaseline for long lasting shine.

To balance uneven lips, use a lighter lip shade on the smaller lip.

Keep your lip colour natural. Lip gloss looks way hotter than lipstick, but it doesn't last as well, so keep it in your bag and reapply throughout the day!

Getting to

You're chillin' out in front of your fave TV show when your best friend calls to invite you out for an all-night party! Do you:

a) Don't even speak to her – let the answerphone take the strain!

b) Explain that you're chillin', but suggest another night instead.

c) You're dressed before she's finished inviting you!

A friend asks you to meet her at 8am – what's your reaction?

a) Don't even speak to her – let the answerphone take the strain!

b) Explain that you're chillin', but suggest another night instead.

c) You're dressed before she's finished inviting you!

Your crush comes over and asks if you'd like to dance. Do you:

a) Agree at once and drag him onto the dance floor – if you're not there already!

b) Agree, but wait for a song you really love.

c) Blush and pretend your shoes hurt!

Someone is wearing the same dress as you. What do you do?

a) You don't even notice – you're having too much fun to care!

b) You're mortified! But there's nothing you can do about it now, so you laugh it off and decide to enjoy the party anyway.

c) Rush home to change – secretly quite glad for the excuse to get back!

Know You!

It's midnight and the music's pumpin'. Your best friend is tearing up the dance floor with her funky moves. Where are you?

a) Right beside her, matching her move for move.

b) Dancing, but with one eye on your watch – it's pretty late!

c) Asleep in the corner.

You've been partying the whole weekend and you're invited out on Monday night for a dancing extravaganza. Do you:

a) Jump at the chance – you can' wait to party again!

b) Politely refuse – you've gotta get some me-time!

c) Refuse point-blank – you've done enough partying this weekend to last you a lifetime!

On Friday night your best friend comes over with a film you've wanted to see for ages. Do you:

a) Persuade her to hit the town – you can watch the film tomorrow!

b) Call up some more friends and make a slumber party of it.

c) Settle down to enjoy the film – you've already got the popcorn ready!

It's summertime and there's a beach party and barbeque, starting at 10pm. How do you react?

a) Groovilicious! Let's hit the sand!

b) Agree to go for a while, as long as you're home for your curfew!

c) 10pm? You're usually tucked up in bed by then!

Answers

Mostly a)s Hey, party animal! No bash is too small – you'll be dancing till dawn! You're great fun, but don't forget that you need to relax sometimes too! Take some time to kick back with a film and some close friends.

Mostly b)s You've got a groovin' balance between partying and pampering! You know when to push the boundaries and when to curl up in your pjs for a chilled-out pampering session!

Mostly c)s Don't you ever hit the dancefloor? It sounds like you'd rather put your feet up than use them for some funky dance moves! Relaxing is important – but keep it in proportion girl! Get out there and show those party animals what you're really made of!

Girls Have

use these ideas to kick-start your creativity and plan your own groovin' party!

Theme
the best parties have a theme! How about a black-and-white party, or a masked bash with prizes for the best mask!

Invitations
you can really have fun with these! Let your imagination go wild. If you've got a theme, use it for the invitations too. Or if it's a small party, how about giving exclusive gifts to your guests?

Décor
think about decorations! If you've got a theme for your party that should help you have some x-treme design ideas!

Food
what snacks are you gonna serve up?

All the Fun

Design your space
don't forget to make room for a dance floor!

Music
– Music's one of the most important features of a sizzlin' party! Plan your sounds in advance and have plenty of CDs on stand-by.

Drinks
serve fruity cocktails or super smoothies!

Entrance
advertise your venue! Lights, balloons or signs will help guests find the party!

Surf's Up!

SPOT THE TEN DIFFERENCES BETWEEN THESE SNAPS OF SASHA AND JADE CHILLIN' AT THE BEACH!

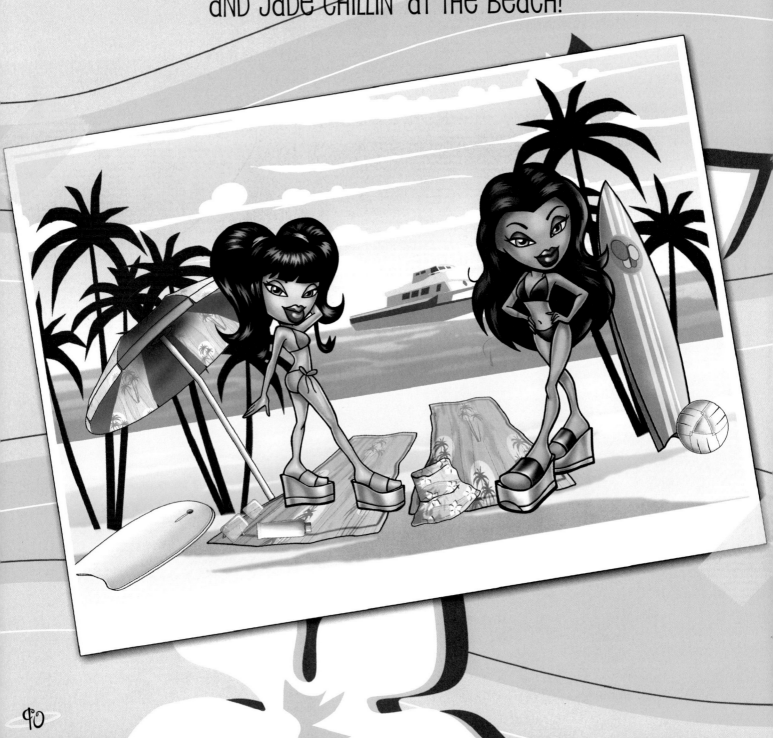

Surf's Up!

SPOT THE TEN DIFFERENCES BETWEEN THESE SNAPS OF SASHA AND JADE CHILLIN' AT THE BEACH!

ANSWERS: 1.BOAT HAS MOVED. 2.PALM TREE MISSING. 3.BODY BOARD IS UPSIDE DOWN. 4.SURFBOARD HAS MOVED. 5.UMBRELLA HAS MOVED DOWN. 6.VOLLEY BALL HAS MOVED. 7.SUNCREAM IS MISSING. 8.HAT HAS MOVED. 9.CLOUD IS MISSING. 10.SUNGLASSES HAVE MOVED.

Sun Kissed Summer

Hi, I'm *Sasha*, and I'm gonna tell you about one of the best days of the whole summer!

We were all round at Meygan's house, trying out the new makeup we'd bought at the mall.

"This new lip gloss is spectacular," I said, brushing the deep red glimmer onto my pouty lips. "The colour is rich to the max."

"I totally love the latest shades", added Jade, slicking some funkalish lime green colour onto her lids.

Cloe ran a comb through her fine blonde hair and then tied it up with a sparkly silver hair clip.

"I picked up some new blush," she said, squeezing in beside me on the dressing table stool. "I can't wait to try it out!"

"What *is* the plan for tonight then, ladies?" enquired Yasmin as Cloe gave her cheeks a delicate rose tint.

Just then the doorbell rang and Meygan went to answer it. There was the sound of voices downstairs, footsteps on the stairs, then Dylan poked his head around the door!

"Hey!" squealed Cloe. "This is a boudoir, boys! Totally sacred!"

"Chill; Meygan said we could come up!" said Cade, shoving Dylan in the back and following him into the room. Cameron and Koby were close behind. "So what's crackin'? We thought we'd slide over here and check if you wanted to groove on out with us tonight?"

"We've been trying to decide what to do," Yasmin told them, crossing her perfectly tanned legs.

"We were thinking about hitting that new club, The Red Corner," said Cameron. "I hear it–"

"Stinks?" I finished for him. "They think hip-hop is a *playground game!*"

"I heard it was rockin'!" Dylan interrupted. "Have you actually *been* there, Sasha?"

"Not exactly," I replied, thinking fast. "But you can hear their low-taste sounds from outside!"

"I think we should check it out," said Koby. "I feel like dancin'!"

"Well I'm with Sasha," Meygan stated. "I don't wanna waste my hours in a total dive!"

"What do you want to do then, ladies?" Cade asked.

Cloe shrugged.

"Allberry's is always laid back and we *know* the music's groovin'."

"Yeah, I could totally devour a couple of their fruit smoothies!" Jade grinned.

"Perfect for a hot summer night!" agreed Yasmin.

Cloe

Cameron, always the peacemaker, gave his irresistible grin. "Ok, I guess we're not gonna agree on the venue right now! But we've got a whole hot summer *day* to cruise through first. What say we split, spend the day havin' fun however we like, and hook up this evening for decision-making?"

"Ok, agreed Cloe. "See you guys later."

Dylan low-fived Cameron and turned to leave.

"Enjoy yourselves at the mall!" called Cade cheekily.

After they'd gone, Jade gave a frown.

"Those guys are getting too smooth for their groove!"

"Yeah, the mall's not the *only* place we have fun!" pouted Cloe.

"So what *are* we gonna do?" asked Yasmin again.

"There's only one place for us when the sun's out and the sky's blue!" said Cloe.

"*The beach!*" we yelled together!

We each went home to collect our beachwear, then congregated by Cloe's Cadillac, checking our makeup in the wing mirrors.

I slid into the passenger seat to check out Cloe's sounds for the ride. Pretty soon we were cruising down the road to the beach, with the music pumping and our hair blowing back in the wind.

"This is the best idea!" enthused Meygan. "It's what summer was made for!"

The ride to the beach was fun, with everyone singing along to the music I picked, but it was awesome to finally see the sun sparkling on the sea. As we were pulling our bags out of the car, we heard a shout and saw Fianna and Nevra waving from the sand dunes.

"We *knew* we'd see you here!" squealed Fianna, shaking back her gleaming brown hair. "It's the only place to be on a day like this – topping up the tan!"

"Definitely!" said Yasmin, grinning. "We're planning to stretch and do some serious sunbathing!"

"Come and join us over here!" Nevra suggested. "We're just a few steps from the beach bar for when we need drinks or snacks!"

"I'm down with that!" said Jade quickly, tucking her funky beach bag under one arm. "Let's do it!"

We joined Meygan and Nevra, and laid out our beach towels in a circle so we could easily chat. In the middle we spread out our high-factor suncream, books and magazines for the day ahead. Then we changed into our bikinis and got ready to tan. I flipped my sunnies down onto my nose – pink tinted with a glittery heart in one corner – ultra-glam!

Sun Block 15

"Our new bikinis are all super-stylin'," said Cloe, flicking lazily through the pages of Jade's fashion mag. "We really zeroed in on the latest colours!"

"Don't we always?" I smiled, enjoying the warmth of the sun playing over my tanned body.

"Whatever the guys are doing, it's no way as cool as this!" Yasmin smirked.

"Koby's probably got them watching his latest video masterpiece!" giggled Jade. But Fianna and Nevra exchanged amused glances.

Yasmin

"'Fraid not, ladies – they arrived a few minutes before you did!" said Fianna, pointing down the beach. We gaped! Koby and Cameron were riding the waves with ease on their surfboards, while Cade was kite-surfin' – speeding along the white sand!

"But I can't see Dylan!" I puzzled.

"That's because he's right behind you!" said a voice, then I was doused in cold sea water!

"*Fox*!" I shrieked, leaping to my feet. "That was icy!"

"Just a bit of fun, Bunny Boo!" he appealed, with his cute grin.

"That's ok," smiled Jade wickedly, "as long as *we* can have a bit of fun too! You look in need of a total makeover, Fox!" She waved her makeup bag at him menacingly and Dylan sprinted back down the beach to join Cade!

"I'm starting to melt!"
murmured Cloe later that morning, after
a long sunbathing session.
"Let's hit the beach bar!" suggested
Meygan. "They make kickin' cool cocktails!"
Everyone got to their feet – all except Jade.
"What's up, Kool Kat?" asked Yasmin, bending down
beside her. Then she gave a little giggle. "She's
fast asleep!"
I nudged Jade gently with my foot and she woke up
with a jump.
"What's going on?"
"Heat too much for you, *Kool Kat?*" I grinned.
"We're heading over to the beach bar – I didn't think
you'd wanna miss out!"

Jade stood up, laughing, and we were soon sitting on high
stools around the kickin'-cool beach bar. The bartender
grinned when he saw us.
"Fruit cocktails all round?" he enquired.
"You know what we like!" crowed Jade.
"And I'll have a slice of
watermelon – I'm
totally in
need
of
some
tasty
rehydration!"
"Mmmm," said
Fianna, sipping her
cranberry and orange mix. "Total pleasure!"
"The weirdest combinations are a taste
sensation!" I agreed as I took a long
drink of my blackcurrant and lime
cocktail.

Jade's watermelon looked so good that we all ordered a slice. But the delicious sticky juice ran down our chins!

"I need to wash this off before it stains my new bikini," groaned Cloe, wiping her mouth delicately.

"Well that's what the ocean's for, ladies!" Yasmin said. "Let's hit the waves!"

We sauntered down the beach, lovin' the feeling of hot sand between our toes, until we reached the sparkling blue water.

"Almost as blue as Angel's eyes!" observed Meygan.

"It's just natural beauty!" giggled Cloe, striking a pose.

"You ladies venturing in to ride the waves?" called a voice, and we saw Koby sitting on his surfboard a little way out to sea. Further out Cameron gave us a quick wave.

"I'm just here for a quick dip," Cloe said, lowering herself slowly into the cool water with a happy sigh. We all followed her in – the water felt fantastic on our hot skin! But Jade swam out to the boys with powerful strokes – and I was right behind her!

"Time to go for a swim, guys!" Jade said as she reached them.

"Yeah, we'll show how to catch a wave!" I added, treading water beside her.

Koby and Cameron passed over their boards and we were soon waiting for the swell!

"You're doing it all wrong!" Koby informed us.

"You'll never make it," Cameron called out. But just then Jade nodded out to sea – she'd seen a wave coming and we were gonna be ready for it! Cameron and Koby were still telling us what we were doing wrong when we caught the wave and sprang into standing position as we rode it in to shore!

"Hey!" spluttered Cameron as he scrambled out of the water after us. "Where'd you learn to surf like that?" "It just comes naturally," I shrugged, handing him back his board.

"You've gotta prove it to groove it," said Jade as she returned Koby's board. "Come on *Bunny Boo*, let's hit the towels!" We walked back to the dunes arm in arm, with Cameron and Koby staring after us in amazement!

The other girls had finished their swim and were already back sunbathing. We laid back and reapplied our sun lotion.

"Sometimes you've just gotta teach those guys a lesson!" smiled Jade as we told the girls about our surfin' triumph.

"But right now I just wanna bronze!" Yasmin sighed happily, crossing her toned arms behind her head and leaning back. "We've got the whole afternoon to tan, girls!"

As the sun sank low in the sky, we saw the guys striding towards us and sat up.

"Awesome day!" crowed Cade. "I'm the king of kite-surfin'!"

"We caught the best waves of the summer!" said Koby, punching the air.

"You ladies had a good day?" asked Dylan, pushing his sunnies onto the top of his head.

"Groovelicious," said Cloe.

"Tanned to the max," Meygan smiled.

"Especially when we showed off our top surfin' talent!" added Jade with a grin.

"Anyway," said Cameron, changing the subject swiftly. "What's the score for tonight?"

"Make up your minds to join us at The Red Corner, ladies," insisted Cade. "It'll be kickin' cool."

"I'd rather lose my passion for fashion!" I said firmly, my hands on my hips.

"We want to go to Allberry's, Blaze," said Cloe, appealing to Cameron with her crystal blue eyes open wide.

"We could do Allberry's?" wavered Cameron, looking at the other guys. But Koby shook his head.

"No way, bro – I'm in the mood to groove!"

It was a total stand-off! There was no way they were getting us into that down-beat club – but it looked like they were gonna be stubborn about our favourite bar café! Then Cloe started to giggle.

"What's the comedy, *Angel?*" I asked.

"Just that it seems there's only one thing we can all agree on – the beach is the **major summer hotspot!** So why do we have to go back into the city at all? We're lovin' it here so much – let's stay and party!"

"Funkalicious!" squealed Fianna.

"Steamin' idea!" Dylan grinned.

"We've got a change of clothes in the car!" I said. "Let's get stylin'!"

Yasmin

While the guys headed for the beach bar, we dashed back to the car and Cloe popped the boot open. When we'd grabbed our evening outfits, she pulled out a half-size mirror, closed the boot and set it on top of the car.

"Beach party beauty salon!" she grinned as we changed into our outfits. With our fresh tans and sparkling eyes, we knew we would look glowing in the evening light!

101

Cloe had pulled on a cute little black dress with a purple lining that peeped out from under the hem, paired with a fringed pink clutch bag. She looked stylin' sweet!

Jade had a sheer purple strapless dress with lighter layers that rippled in the gentle sea breeze. The colour made her green eyes shine! Then Meygan emerged in her outfit.

"What do you think?" she giggled, giving a twirl. "Totally hot, Fashion Monkey!" exclaimed Cloe. Meygan's dress was hot and hip! A diagonal-cut green halter neck with a matching bag slung over her arm.

"Princess, you look royal!" I said, admiring Yasmin's tiger print red dress with her strappy black sandals.

I was pleased with my own look too – a dusty blue flare skirt dress with a funkalish cowl neck and a low-slung belt to accentuate my hips!

We squeezed together around Cloe's DIY dressing table and applied a fresh layer of makeup. With our sunkissed skin we didn't need much! Just a slick of gloss and a dusting of eye shadow, and we were ready to rock!

Cloe

Jade

Meygan

luscious lip gloss

102

The beach bar was staying open late, but when we got back there the guys were looking totally dejected!

"What's eatin' you?" asked Cloe in concern.

"There's no music," grumbled Cade. "The bar hasn't got a boom box! No dancing tonight!"

But Cloe grabbed my arm and grinned.

"No worries," she stated. "Sasha's got the mix and I've got the stereo!"

I soon figured out what she meant! I helped her back the Cadillac up to the beach bar, then picked out a selection of my favourite hip hop beats! Her car's music centre did the rest!

"Jumpin'!" laughed Cameron, starting to move to the groove! Soon we were all on our feet, slicin' sand!

"This is way cooler than Allberry's!" giggled Fragrance.

"And the sounds totally top The Red Corner!" Dylan admitted.

"Hey, just call me your own personal DJ!" I grinned.

The bar tender created some totally rad fruit cocktails and we stopped dancing just long enough to sip them and cool down!

"We've got our own club right here on the sand!" Meygan laughed.

"Don't let's waste the dancin' time!" cried Cade, pulling her to her feet!

"It's the sound of summer!" I cheered, joining them. And we danced all evening!

Yasmin

Sasha

103

Sasha's Tips for a

AT THE START OF SUMMER WE GIRLS CAN'T WAIT TO CRUISE DOWN TO THE BEACH. BUT DON'T LET THAT SUN, SEA AND SAND MAKE YOU FORGET ABOUT YOUR BEAUTY ESSENTIALS!

Hair – Sun and sea water can do your hair a lot of damage! Make sure you have a deep treatment conditioner to use over the summer months.

Rub hair-protecting serum through to the ends of your hair, then tie it into a ponytail before you hit the beach. Wrap a piece of funky fabric or colourful ribbon around the hair band for a fashion forward look.

Sun lotion – Always use a high SPF at the start of the summer, and don't forget to protect your lips with a sunscreen. Apply your lotion before you hit the beach, and reapply after a swim!

Sun Block 15

Sun-Kissed Summer

Eyes – Don't forget to cover your eyes with some ultra-hip sunnies – they'll keep your eyes feelin' fresh and protect you from the sun's powerful rays.

Nails – Sand and water can play havoc with your nailcare routine! Keep your nails looking good with regular manicures and pedicures.

Bikini – Just because you're relaxin', no need to abandon your natural style! Pick your bikini carefully to match your colouring and body shape.

Solids are really hip – check out bright colours like pink, green or turquoise. Or pick retro patterns and vintage styles.

If you're very slim, try a halter neck top with a boy leg bottom to add curves. If you're a little larger try a bandeau top and high-cut bottoms. Lookin' good, girl!

Cool Cocktails

TRY SOME OF OUR FAVOURITE FRUITY COCKTAILS!

Honey Cocktail

100ml apple juice
100ml orange juice
Juice of 1/2 a lime
2 teaspoons of honey

Shake and strain into glasses

Gentle Sea Breeze

2 parts cranberry juice
2 parts pineapple juice

Shake and strain into glasses filled with crushed ice
Garnish with a sprig of mint

Virgin Mary

Ice
300ml of tomato juice
2 drops Tabasco
(or more if you like it hot!)
1 teaspoon of horseradish sauce
Juice of 1/2 of a lemon

A dash of salt and pepper
Shake and strain into ice-filled highball glasses!

Coco

2 cups of pineapple juice
1 cup of coconut milk
A handful of ice

Blend and pour into chilled glasses

Greek Goddess

4 parts peach juice
2 parts orange juice
1 part lemon juice
A handful of ice

Blend together and serve garnished with fresh fruit!

Cinderella

2 parts pineapple juice
2 parts orange juice
2 parts lemon juice

Strain over ice cubes and top up with soda water Garnish with a pineapple chunk and a cherry on a stick!

Beach Babe

15 ways to make sure you stand out from the crowd!

Bikini – You're gonna be wearin' it the whole summer so make sure it's flattering and comfortable!

Lips – Apply plenty of lip protection cream – the sun can really dry out your pout!

Swimming – Try and keep your hair out of the water while you're swimming and don't linger in the ocean too long – the wrinkled prune look is not a hot one!

Sun lotion – Keep reapplying your lotion throughout the day. You're not just protecting against harmful rays – the skin has a totally ageing effect on skin.

Sun Block 15

Hair – Keep your hair lookin' luscious – cover up with a sun hat or a stylin' headscarf for easy chic!

Drink – Take a super-sized bottle of water with you – the sun really sucks moisture and you need to replenish, girl!

Surfing – Why not try something new this summer? Learn how to surf, or try body boarding with your best friends.

Sunglasses – The delicate skin around your eyes can burn way too easily! Take the opportunity to don some really groovin' sunnies!

Wraps – The beach opens up a whole new fashion passion! Floaty wraps in shimmery fabrics or cooling cottons are a must when you need to cover up!

Pick the right beach – Every beach is different! Figure out what you're gonna want from a beach – do you dig plenty of activities, or would you prefer a more exclusive hard-to-find spot?

After-sun – Don't forget about your beauty routine when you leave the beach! Keep your skin glowing with some aftersun lotion, and wash the sand out of your hair carefully. Let your hair dry naturally – blitzing with heat could damage your locks. And that wavy beach hair look is the summer's latest style sensation!

After Sun

Beach pack – If your summer's gonna be spent on the beach, why not create your own beach pack and keep it ready to go! As well as your beachwear and towel, don't forget sun lotion, hair serum, a spare outfit and, of course, your makeup bag! Take plenty of magazines or books, and don't go without your mobile if you're meeting friends on the sand!

Shade – Take a couple of big sun umbrellas and dig them into the sand to create some shady areas. The mid-day sun can be powerful and you want to look buff, not burned!

Music – Who's the DJ in your group? We never hit the beach without some pumpin' sounds – and I'm always on top of the mix! Take along a boom box and plenty of your favourite CDs.

Exercise – Kickin' back on a towel in the sun and chatting is always fun, but if you're buzzin' with energy why not start a game of beach volleyball? You'll improve your all-over sports tan, and it's a great way to meet new friends!